NOTES FROM THE JOURNEY WESTWARD

Notes
from the
Journey Westward

Joe Wilkins

White Pine Press PoetryPrize Volume 17

White Pine Press / Buffalo, New York

Acknowledgments:
Alaska Quarterly Review: "Theodicy [On her way to the mission school...]"
The Adirondack Review: "Anniversary [Three trees back of the old house...]"
Beloit Poetry Journal: "Hayrake," "Notes from the Journey Westward"
Blackbird: "Route 7 Outside Nacogdoches, Texas"
Briar Cliff Review: "Bread and Butter"
Boxcar Poetry Review: "The Voice of the Father"
Cave Wall: "One More Time Durango," "The Old Ways Fade and Do Not Come Back"
Cutthroat: "Reckoning"
Devil's Lake: "Radio All Night Special AM"
Evergreen Review: "Manifesto"
Fiddlehead: "Seven Devils"
The Fourth River: "Right Now"
The Georgia Review: "Anniversary [Together, we were tough enough...]"
Acknowledgments continue on page 112.

First Edition

Cover art: Edith Freeman, "Creek Bottom," 1980–1991, woodcut.
Collection of the Yellowstone Art Museum, Billlings, Montana;
Montana Collection, gift of the Edith Freeman Estate. 1993.004.

ISBN 978-1-935210-36-8

Printed and bound in the United States of America

Library of Congress Control Number: 2012931168

Published by
White Pine Press
P.O. Box 236
Buffalo, NY 14201
www.whitepine.org

For my mother—
thank you isn't enough.

Notes from the Journey Westward

We drove that car as far as we could,
abandoned it out west.

—Bob Dylan

He Devil

Listen Mister Lightning Catcher,
you old stone buzzard
with your red head of rocks
& rocks for feathers,
I'm damn tired of remembering
you. You say: I will teach you
mountains. Get down from there.
I don't need that kind
of dignity. The music in your bones
is scree & stone, off-key, old.

Hardscrabble Prairie Triptych

——*Follow Me*

I know a place where barb-wire
wreathes the heaped bones of horse.
I know where we can shoulder our bright

rifles and bag a twine string
of rabbits. It's out past the alkali basin,
right in the dark yawn of that sod-roof shack.

——*It'll Get You Every Time*

See how gravel breathes the river?
How water slows and pools, now begins
to stink? I pull mussels from their nests of mud,

you work a quick knife clean
through each. There's nothing to be done
about hope. See, no matter the stories there's never

any pearls. We crack them open
anyway, shells bright as a boy's eyes,
scoop out each stinking handful of meat.

——*Back to the Land*

Like the lovely drunk
at the Antlers we so admired,
with his blue suit and cloud bright hat,

the land here falls flat
on its back. Just dust and blue grass
and a wind bearing up dry rivers of sky.

Notes from the Journey Westward

We died in the wagon. We had been sick
        since Wyoming, since the skin
of things had begun to pock
        with sagebrush and knobs of rock,
like the wrecked face of that bare-
        knuckle man back in Cincinnati.

We said our little prayers. In our fever
        the angels came. They had no teeth.
Tongues thick as snakes, sky-wide
        mouths, lips cracked as ours—
in this dry place, we decided,
        even the seraphim must thirst.

We ate the meat they gave us
        and were hungry. We drank the milk
and were thirsty. We pissed where we lay
        and did not understand. Yet we asked
no questions. We knew the only answer
        was farther West.

And here is what they did: Above a dry valley,
        up under a sandstone ledge,
they shoveled us in. If it weren't for the blood,
        our snapped and lolling bones,
dust the wagon left settling on our lips,
        we might have had the look of lovers.

Once, we were given an orange. This was early,
        just across the Missouri, the grass
thick, green willows weeping along the creeks.
        We would still walk then, a minute

here or there, hand on a horse's muscled rump.
        And at the very hour of our death, again
we tasted it, how we ate it peel and all.

Mission School, 1922: What She Remembered

That for a winter's share of months—
which felt then to her like years—
teacher shut the schoolhouse doors.

That one day sunlight dazzled the still snow-blue mountains.
That it was nearly freezing but for the light
it seemed the day was warm.

That she found digging in the creek bank with a dull axe
a frog frozen as a stone, not a beat left
in its still bright heart.

That even in the brace of April, on her way to school again,
the wind's hard blade bit to the bloody quick
her old horse's hocks and belly.

That one tight knot of ice at a time the creek
came unstuck. That all day it pulled and snapped—
like pine burls in a fire,
like gunshots for no reason in the night,
like the marrow bones mother Warman broke between her teeth.

That at recess the Warman boys would steal potatoes
and kisses, chase her until her head spun,
her good heart heaving with the burn and throb
of blood. How she loved it—

the three of them back of the clapboard school,
mineral smell of snowmelt and mountain,
lick of government grease down a still-warm potato.

How her own body warmed as the world warmed,
how like riding home in the whole-sky spill of spring rain
there was no clean line between her and it.

How finally it was rain, not snow.
How when the creek slid back into its channel they found both boys
tangled naked in the roots of a cottonwood, how on the flood grass
they laid them out like fish. How they were their bodies,

how they were not their bodies,
how the hearts of boys do not freeze but fill.

How on the way to school she rode
by mother Warman, wailing near cottonwoods,
notching her wrists and shoulders. How those May mornings
her old horse loved more than anything

the hearts of plum flowers. How teacher made the Crow girls wash
with lye their lousy hair. How they screamed. That for days after

their scalps were white as snow.

Theodicy

On her way to the mission school
my grandmother saw
how they'd put the Warman boys up
in the crook of a cottonwood—
wrapped them in skins,
tied old boards to their backs,
and put them up in a cottonwood.

That was *1923* and the Crow
were dying. That was down on the Big Horn,
my grandmother, just seven years old,
riding a paint horse
up the creek's dry wash,
where she turned north each day,
where that morning mother Warman
sat in the dirt and weeds and wailed,
tore at the skin of her neck and arms,
watched this little white girl come by,
alive. My grandmother's eyes

see nothing now.
Her hair a white confusion,
skin the color of driftwood,
face a dry wash. *Whatever it is,*
she says to me, lost again in story,
you must love it. As you come naked
from the river, let the wind kiss
and shiver you. There will be boys in the trees,
women taking strips of their own skin.
I don't know if there is a God,
but stay alive. Be sad awhile.
Stay alive.

Weathering

A cowbird pecks at the frozen edge
of a reservoir. The thin ice cracks.

A man throws the last flakes of hay
from the back of a flat-bed Ford.

The chewing cattle steam with heat.
The day is bright as dried bone.

Cottonwoods let go their breath
of wind, and a scrim of snow leaps

across the prairie. The cowbird
caws. In the cab the man wipes

frost from his beard, pours coffee
from a thermos, then reaches

into a brown paper bag and lifts out
two golden biscuits. The cowbird

wings its way to sky. The man says
a prayer for empty gizzards and eats.

Names on the Land

Freeze Out Notch

The breath of mountains
is dry grass and sloped fields
of winter wheat. Their eyes
are bedrock and ice.

Clearwater Canyon

Old men drink tall glasses
of yellow beer and stare
at themselves in the mirror.

Trailer Hollow

A red-winged blackbird
hops across the hood
of a red pickup.

Hog Meadows

She dips a bucketful
of creek water and runs
laughing back to her father.
Look, he says and points
to the pail's rippling
mouth, *the sky!*

Comanche Flats

Dust settles in the draws
and canyons
of your skin,
the lakes of your eyes.

Colt-Killed Creek

Ten-thousand butterflies
stream up the rocks—
a bright river run the wrong way.

Paradise Ridge

Cedar burns quick and hot.
The house was a breath
of ash before anyone got there.

Amos Bench

Now, he thinks,
as the tractor crests
the hill, *I'll swath
the sky.*

William T. Phillips

The theory is that Butch Cassidy did not die in a shootout in Bolivia in *1908*, but assumed a new name, William T. Phillips, and lived a quiet life in Spokane until his death in 1937.[...] A long, rambling manuscript written by the elderly Phillips entitled *The Bandit Invincible* [...] purports to be a biogarphy of Cassidy. [...] The manuscript also lapses, briefly, into the first person."
  —Jim Kershner, Inland Northwest History blog at
  The Spokesman Review, a Spokane, Washington, daily paper.

At noon, he combs his mustache and puts on his bowler hat and walks down the littered avenue to the lunch counter on the corner. It's noisy, the tables filthy. The woman brings him meatloaf, always meatloaf, because he pays with stories. He used to sell dictionaries door to door, but now his old bones clack like dominoes in a cedar box and he can no longer bear the weight of all those words. So, it's a good thing he doesn't mind meatloaf, it's a good thing the waitress here is lonely too and loves his stories. He tries to be very careful. He will say things like, *When he rode up the canyon, the night was big and dark and far to the stars.* He will say, *Butch loved dogs. He had a yellow dog named Sunday he loved very much. He almost didn't leave the country when they wouldn't allow Sunday on the ocean liner. Near the end of his life, Butch pined mostly for that old dog.* And later, after the woman has brought him a second cup of coffee and he has thanked her and tipped his once fine hat and she has smiled and shuffled away, he walks down the hill to the river. There is a park there where most days he sits for a bit and thinks. Sometimes a stray will come sniffing out of the willows and he will call to it. He loves dogs. He knows that much for sure. Yet in the evening, the sun dying over the pines, the mountains going blue and dark, he waits for stars that never look right, he says to himself the names—*Old Bert, Kid Curry, Sundance, Sundance, Sundance*—that sound so exquisite and wrong. The street he lives on is paved. He sleeps above a watchmaker's shop, all those tiny gears and bells. He is nearly seventy years-old in this city of coal smoke and automobiles. What did he do to deserve this? What did he do? What did he do? He doesn't know. He walks back to his room. He gets out a piece of rolled tin and a sheet of paper, loads his old pearl-handled Colt and sets it on his desk. Now he dips the bent point of the tin into a bowl of blue ink and writes: *Butch knew he'd lived a good life. He was kind to women. He always had a shiny new jack-knife for a boy. And that day, the sun bearing down, the dust of the road thick in the dry air, the whole Bolivian Army waiting outside, he wasn't scared. Six-guns blazing, I stepped out to meet them.*

Devil's Throne

I call this place Kingdom Come,
or Cutthroat Hook, maybe
Devil's Throne: a rocky saddle
between bowls of rock & frost-stunted pine.
The only bones here, of course, are bright
white & warm today in sun
& wind, & can you see
the smoke of my breakfast fire
write a story for a moment in the sky?

The Sheep Shearers

A distinct culture has evolved out of the practice of shearing sheep.
—Wikipedia entry

All long necks and whiskers and three-day hangovers
sweated out on the peeling linoleum of some low-slung camper,
all greasy jeans and pearl snapshirts undone to the belly,
all black coffee and cigarettes and potted meat—

no one respectable, that's for sure,
though come March, it wasn't about respectable.
From behind the old sofa, you watched Johnny Ahern
sprawl in a chair at the kitchen table,

wet trail of snoose dripping from his frog's chin—
your mother fed him three kinds of pie,
your father shook his gnarled hand—
hand that could take a sheep to skin

in seconds—and said, *Thanks for coming, Johnny.*
Lord and the devil know we need you.

*

Skinny as a barn cat, the one that knocked on the door
and came in for chamomile tea and a visit with your mother.
Her face was square and small, a ribbon of scar
from ear to chin, and after her small cup she rolled

a cigarette, tapped the ash into her palm. She was one of those
that could have been twenty-three or forty-two. No matter,
what you remember most is how her straw hair
was pulled back with flowers. It was yet mid-winter.

She must have grown them in whichever
rusted Airstream she called home, carried them in her lap
through a thousand icy miles of mountain two-lane,
set them in the sink after the table was broke down

into a marriage bed. And now, ringing her wrecked face—
umber buds, filigree of leaf, a crown of wild rose.

*

Milk-faced and bare-chested, trousers gone to threads,
they stood in a ragged line and stared at you.
You stared back. They didn't speak but turned and ran
to the river. So, you followed. Picked up a rock,

like they did, and winged it at a carp. Together,
you floated a hunk of cottonwood to the far bank,
set a muskrat trap, jostled and laughed, and when the sheep
were sheared—the men gone into town for liquor,

women gathering dogs and laundry—
you sat on the steps and worked river mud
from between your toes, felt with each breath the bluing bruise
on your chest, where, after she threw you to the ground,

that dark-eyed shearer's girl propped a knee to pin you
and kissed you hard on the mouth.

Prairie Heritage Museum, Culbertson, Montana

It was late, distended sky gone bruise blue,
the very air ready for some flood,
and I had hours yet to drive. And hours lost
already in room after room of life-sized
historical dioramas, then a fifty minute lecture,
vis-à-vis who knows what, delimiting
the days of dairy farmers from those of beef farmers.

A farmer forty years myself, he'd said,
and you could see the settling dust of him—
left hip a no-good trick, warped board of his back,
even his one good eye a bit unmoored.
His dentures clacked as he laughed,
as he put his trembling hand to my shoulder
and walked me out the museum's back door

and across the gravel lot. The wind was hard
and dark, but the caboose was beautiful—
I'll give him that. Abandoned over by the abandoned
grain elevator when B&N tore out the tracks in '82,
the caboose had been a home for hobos and drifters—
which he hated to see. *You see,* he said,
out here on the prairie we don't have much

but our heritage. So, last spring,
since no one knew who really owned the thing,
I just called up Bud Wilson's boy—
this he told me as if all men surely must know Bud—
and had him fire up his flatbed and haul this here
old caboose the hell on over to the museum.
He was beaming, his old back straightening.

I sanded slats and buffed rust all summer.
Just last week I finally painted it, like it used to be,
cherry red and coal black—and just then the black sky
gave way: a purling wind snapped grass, slapped rain
against our faces. Like drifters we climbed on in.
For what little light there was we let the door swing
and clatter. What a clattering across the walls:

here, four dark riders spurring wolves;
there, a many-handed, bone-backed beast
with two long tongues; and, finally, the whore,
M16'd armies crawling from between her bloody knees—
and around them and us, in a script so neat and tidy
even the schoolmarm mannequin
from the museum diorama might approve,

wrapped the good book's record of these last days—
save above the sink, where the strokes began to spin
and twist, the lurch of them like watching
rain, one particular raindrop: I *have seen I have seen*
I have I have seen all I have seen. And the old man said
nothing, as if of this itinerant's scrawl there was nothing
to explain, as if the slip and suck of his dentures

at his gums was all that was necessary for sense,
as if what mattered was not what was before us,
but what he'd already explained—
say the way with steel-wheeled steam tractors
they first broke this earth; how rain here
comes sometimes dryly, a storm above
and not a drop below; how in that drought in '61

the dairies hereabouts fed their cows flax flowers
and the milk went blossom blue; or when
on the Tacoma run the engineers switched shifts,
and the tired one washed from his face the coal-soot here,
in this caboose, maybe caught a nap; how we forget
or get wrong what God did or didn't say—
but remember rain, grass, an hour's rest.

Then I Packed You Up the Ridge
Like a Brother on My Back

In the blue dark I followed the ridge
toward the pines.

In a bowl of sage and dry grass
soft as the throat-hairs

of something small,
I lay down.

The sun was a long time coming,
the earth bloodless at my belly.

I waited and watched the river.
I was very still. You know how it is—

the stars closing their bright mouths,
the dew a gift on your lips.

You did not see me,
or my rifle,

blue as the dark. I saw you
step from the willows,

give your nose to the black water.
And you were beautiful. There is so much

blood in a thing—
yours welled up from the clean hole

I made in your heart and steamed
on the river stones,

and some washed down into the river,
where it swirled a moment,

and became the breath of fish.

Hayrake

In that interminable summer of the devil's own breath
        it was most all I did:
pull the hayrake behind the old Ford tractor,
        the arced cutter bars

spread wide, the circled forks spinning behind,
        gathering two, sometimes
three thin windrows of drought-shocked alfalfa
        and buffalo grass

together, funneling the sallow, bird-boned, orphan fruit
        of that unpromised land
into a single windrow that wound the field thick enough
        for the bailer to jaw up.

But too: that was the summer of Kevin, my older sister's
        thick-necked,
ridiculous boyfriend. God, but we loved him—
        his jacked-up Toyota

with the iridescent silver roll bar, his Wintermint Skoal
        and seraphic vocabulary
of whistles and grunts. Kevin was from two towns
        over, the county seat,

was something new, something to set against the neighbors:
        the broken old ones,
the sad fat ones, the ones eating each night boiled mudfish
        and boxed mac and cheese,

the ones with names that could have been the names
        of tractors or weeds,

say Harlan Wilson or Sandy Russell, their skinny wives
      and gap-toothed girls,

boys bromidic as their fathers. And all of them, and us,
      dust-stunned, debt-ridden,
just barely hanging on to the sagebrush plains we worked,
      that worked us. Not Kevin:

he was off to play football for the community college;
      without asking
he'd flip the dial to FM, throw his massive fists in the air
      when Van Halen came on;

he wore his sunglasses even inside. So the day I heard
      that Kevin's beautiful
Toyota had like some strange bird lifted him into the dark,
      and he, like my father

and Sandy Russell and Harlan's baby girl, was dust—
      I left the house
and walked north, to the one decent field we had left,
      where I fired the Ford

and turned myself around that patch of dirt for hours, until all
      those skinny windrows
were one and good, and there was only one world,
      and God's or not,

I was in it, and I was pulling the iron-winged hayrake.

Anniversary

Together, we were tough enough to take it. The cheerleaders snickering, those boys leering, coach's rolled eyes. See, I read too many books and couldn't hit a thing from anywhere on the court. And you were too kind to girls who weren't pretty and spent most of your days sharpening new pencils down to stubs in the special-ed classroom. So we stuck together. Like that party down on Bascom Creek, when Jimmy Dickson asked if you got it from your mom or your dad, the retardation, and I picked up a full can of beer and slung it hard and hit Jimmy square in the jaw. I'm as proud of that as anything. And once, driving out to the oil wells to smoke pilfered cigarettes, the day after Christmas, the sun going down over the ice-wracked river, you told me not to worry that they called me faggot and book fucker.

Later, after I stopped coming home summers from college, we started writing letters. Most of mine just showed up back in my campus box after a few weeks, because you moved so much. You always used a marker and began yours with "Dear Friend." I remember one was about a girl you said you were in love with, you said she was only fifteen but was what you really needed. You must have been twenty-two, twenty-three, by then. I think that was the year you buried your brother. And I know—by buried I mean unloaded the still-smoking shotgun and wrapped a bed-sheet around what was left of his head before your mother saw what he'd done to himself.

Last winter, when I was back in town to visit my grandparents, you came by to meet my wife. There were bits of wrapping paper on the floor, long ribbons the color of wine. You were even heavier, your arms sun-dark, the backs of your hands all cut-up and scabbed. We sat in the front room and talked. You'd asked did I remember that blond girl from Belgrade, the one with, you know, the big tits—then suddenly your wide mouth went slack, your pocked face strangely shapeless, and you fell asleep mid-sentence. You slept for hours.

And this is what I really want to talk about: When you woke, we were getting dinner ready. I brought you a glass of water, asked if you wanted to stay. You blinked, licked your thick lips. "I don't know what the fuck I'm doing here," you said. "I've got to be in fucking Roundup." I asked again if you didn't have time to stay. We were looking at each other and not looking at each other. I had thought there might still be something between us. An understanding, maybe. That was vanity. You wiped your mouth on a pillow, got up, and left.

Anniversary

A long time ago now,

rageful and drunk,

I drove hell-bent down the highway
ninety miles an hour or so—

it was April,
the ice on the river breaking up,
sparrows scavenging the puddles,

what the fuck did I think I was doing?
With my fist I hammered
on the trailer door, yelled for you.

Your father answered,
in his yellowing t-shirt and undershorts.
He eyed me, scratched himself,
told me to go home. So I did.
And that was it,

for love anyway—
I was eighteen and the-hell-out-of-there soon,
sure in all matters it was just this wrong
world, that I was right. And we both knew

you'd never leave. Goddamnit,

you were sixteen and slender
and kept wrecking
your thin hips against mine.
What the hell was I supposed to do?

I think I nearly killed us.
At least I hope
you are still alive. Anyway,

now I am telling you I am a small bird,
dun-colored, nervous, rising

again, slamming again
my face against the glass. See there—
blue sky. A hard world away.

Fog

I drove through you, and out of you, and the world then
was lit like it's usually lit—winter trees bright
and black, their shadows black as well, the bright

and dirty snow in the ditch. A moment ago, I couldn't see
a thing. Yet now the tin siding on that lonely warehouse winks
and glisters, the dark graffiti cries so clearly: *Forever my life.*

Once, long ago, I sat on the front-room floor and stared
at the wreck of my father in his easy chair—his bald
and flaking head, red fist of face, chest collapsing

with the sound of a broken bone. He opened his eyes.
"What the hell are you looking at?" he asked. "What's wrong
with you?" I was nine. I left. I don't remember him alive again.

Mount Baal

This is where bear grass
dances twenty ways
in a wind that shifts the skulking cedars,
rolls lake water to the sky. Hang on
to your hat. Here, a man listens
to his own loneliness: his words
ride their windy way back
to his ears, he hears himself
say, Grass, cedar, father, wind.
Then he hears it again.

One More Time Durango

Afternoons, the wide sky a world
of white hammers, anvils, the rare
and unseasonable face,
she grieves hard as iron—
not for him, but for that one good day.
Durango, the mountains hammering

the known world with winter—
feet of blown snow and windows tight with ice—
he's home from work, the cold knives of it
across his face—
and it was his face, hot with blood
and love, how he tumbled
to his knees. Durango. She sees it now

as he must have—
the two of them wrapped in wool
on a pine-chair he hammered months ago—
his months-old daughter,
little wet face of sweat and milk,
and his slender wife's bare
and swollen breasts. All this. And the Durango

cactus on the windowsill, red-veined burst of pearl—
such an unseasonable, messy blossom—
the good stink of it
like milk-soap, like iron.

Moving West

Miss Clarice was probably still sniffling on the step,
waving her kerchief and calling for Earl Wright
to come snip our magnolias for her kitchen table,
but still—I thought we'd never get out.
                              First, the river—
wide as I ever remember, a great bend dividing earth
from earth and sky. Then it was Arkansas, a four lane mess
and hot all day. Just like the South to give such glory
and piss you off all the same.
                              But the sun softened
on the coal hills south of Kansas City. You were tired
and the motel keeper kind—he gave us a cut rate
with a window to the western sky.
                              And we danced
with tall grass, wind, and sunrise, drove the next day a two-lane that slid
like a lover across the plain. The land went blue with spring flax,
until the sky turned black near Valentine, Nebraska.
                              We sheltered
near a schoolhouse, read Stafford to one another. Your breath
was on my face. I heard you say, *This is what I wanted,*
a life like this in the rain.

Testimonial

With faces licked by pine fire, cigarettes flaring in their lips,
these were *Bums, Derelicts, Vagrants!* my grandmother
would have said, and I knew what she meant—
dirty men who never settled, who left their families
and their faith to hitch rides and steal and eat cold beans
straight from the can and what a sad thing
for their poor grandmothers.
                    Yet what I remember most
about that night in a fire-lit rock cave north of the Bull Mountains,
when I was fourteen and my brother thirteen and we snuck away
from church camp and found their camp,
                        was how
they shifted over in the dirt, told us we could sit, if we liked,
how that pine fire popped with sap, how the bottle came
our way, how warm and easy it went down—
                        was how
they leaned into everything: cigarettes and stories, nips of whiskey,
laughter like blackbirds rising across a white sky.

Mother and Child Diptych

Now that she is alone,
she walks to the river each evening

and throws in four stones.
She doesn't know why.

Some days they are for her children,
some days her husband. But today,

they are for that boy
she barely knew but kissed anyway
under the bleachers one recess.

***

He stares at his soggy Cheerios.
He would rather pancakes, a hard fried egg,
chokecherry syrup.

But his mother is still in her slip,
curling her red hair for work.

And his father laid down on the sofa
three months ago and died. So,

he sneaks his bowl
over to the sugar drawer.

The Voice of the Father

Often, as mother bent her slender back
to the fields, or pulled the bloody slip
of a lamb into the world,
I wandered the house,
studying motes of dust brought to life
by sunlight. I was looking for you.

And though you were near—
in the picture on the piano, in the looping
scrawl on your old calendar, in that finger's width
of black hair tucked in an envelope
by mother's bed—I never found you,
never opened the door
that led to the cool room where you knelt
with your rag, where the polished wood of rifles
gleamed and the soap smell of oil
laddered the air.

                    Yet you spoke to me.
When I climbed the piano bench
and wiped dust from the glass, you said, *Look,*
I charm the great dark bird from the sky,
I wear a tie and hold your mother at the waist,
I am this perfect hand of cards.

When I pulled the calendar from the wall
and rubbed my grubby fingers across your script,
you said, *See the price of lambs last year,*
get a nickel better. The battery in the Ford should last
until you're fourteen. For the best meat,
drop a doe after the first frost.

                                    And when I snuck
into mother's lonely room of rumpled sheets, opened
the yellow envelope, and touched to my lips
your clipped black lock, you said,
I have left you.

Fist/Boy/Man/War

3.19.2003

By moonlight we bled—
his skewed nose, my twice-smiling lip,
our alien and offending

hands. How odd they'd looked
in the moon's odd eye—
all one-hundred-eight delicate bones

fisted into four bone-white, artless bludgeons.
It shouldn't be so easy.
Something hard should hold hands

open—some tendon, some ligament, something
working against the idiot heart,
especially the idiot hearts of boys,

who grow up to be men.

Bull Mountain Elemental

Earth

When you leave the fields,

                                    it's in your mouth,
your throat, summer sweater for your tongue—
that taste of roots
                  and shit and iron. You work it
with a jackknife from beneath your nails,
scrub gullies of it at your elbows.
How it becomes your face—
                          wet nostril ring,
furrows of it fanning from the raw wells of your eyes.
Blink and cry but this earth is all
you'll ever see.

Fire

It begins in the rotten body of a cottonwood.
The jackpines too are tinder-dry. Like old women
stepping from the kitchen
                         they sigh and fall
in the bright flames. The rimrocks fairly rage.
Even the valley's a hive of smoke.
For there is no river.
                  Only a track of dust.
Late August and fire everywhere—
river willow and prairie thistle,
dry earth and drier sky,

the coal-hot sacks of your lungs.

Air

A dry wind laves these plains,
lifts and carries

                         the stink of sage and wild onion,
breath of diesel, cries of faraway birds—
and you and I as well.
                                  We unbend
our backs, lift our arms, let the day's sweat whistle dry
down the length of us.
                        Tongue of wind
to bless us, carry us somewhere else.

Water

I wake in the dark.
Only the moon's far eye,
                                    the mouths of stars.
The mud of the field sucks at my hip boots,
a snake swings through alfalfa.

When the sun rises this field will steam
and snakes twist beneath rocks,
                                    and everything
will go down to dust. Yet tonight the ditch

is a runnel of sky—
I step into the moon.

The Twin Imps

For eighteen years you were good
dirty boys: faces ringed
with mud, the sandbox flooded,
mother's bent spoons & that egg-sucking dog's
sucked eggs. Who told you
you could leave? You must know
it's killing all her bones—
the way the sun leaves the mountains:
cold, completely.

Waffle House Parking Lot, Yazoo City, Mississippi

Of course they're here,
this knot of sneering,
droop-eyed teens, and that rusted

Impala you can't believe
they all crawled out of. Where else
would they go? Mosquitos, treefrogs—

drinking up what life they can find,
calling again and again into the night
even when there is no answer.

Drought

Remember it was the world
that went wrong—

your grandmother kicking dust
in the fields, the wind setting it against

your lips. Taste again the dry grass,
see your little brother rolling

naked in the gravel, old collie dog
laid out by the cedar tree.

Remember—this time he won't
get up, not even to piss.

There's your mother sitting
at the kitchen table. She doesn't say

anything, you're not supposed
to touch her. Now mosquitoes

ring the dog's eyes. Your brother
piles dust and dead grass

on his head. Remember—
it was the world. Remember—

the rifle against your shoulder felt good,
you aimed just behind the ear.

This time, don't turn away
from your brother's bird mouth,

the sun on his pink skin. This time,
just tell him to close his eyes.

Theodicy

Stars like you've never seen stars.

I mean it.

We were some miles out on the far prairie—
a track of gravel we called a road,
little tufts of bunch grass, pear cactus,
sage blue-silver and burled,

a dry creek sweeping down from the hills,
the cutbank we leaned up against.

And that burn of stars—

I'm telling you they were the seraphim's choir of true light.
Bright, I'm telling you. Light like God's good
word, his native tongue,

his one fiery, sanctified song in the dark.

We split between the four of us—
we were eleven then, or maybe Carlo was just ten—
that backpack full of warm beers we'd filched
from Cash Franzel's old man,

who we knew would wake tomorrow afternoon
hungover and shit-dumb as ever,
chasing snakes, sure he'd drunk it himself.

Anyway, we did what we were supposed to do—

we chugged suds, we laughed, we spoke words not fit

to be words. Laughed some more. Bill and I clambered
up the cutbank and stood at the dirt lip of it,
our little peckers in our hands.

There, we pissed perfect, crystalline arcs
out into that enkindled night—

and down over Carlo and Cash,
both pawing by starlight the glossy tits of some centerfold.
Do you see what I'm saying?

Strike us down. You might as well. A few years later
Bill quit school and dedicated himself to methamphetamine.
Cash ended up in Iraq. He is still in Iraq.
He fucking loves it there.

And Carlo—
who if I get right down to it was probably just ten,
who beneath his right eye had this sloppy
jackknife scar that slid down his cheek
and went red and loud near his ear—
who knows about Carlo.

I know about the stars.
That night they made shadows of us,
made us bigger, wilder than we were—

blue-silver as the sage,
edged as the creek's steep cutbank,
more alive, more holy, closer by far to God
than any-goddamn-thing-else out there—

grass, pear cactus, rot-wood tumble of a homesteader's shack,
the far-off, sorry, star-strangled lights of the crossroads town
we called home—

they loved us, those stars.

They must have, anyway, for they did
what no one did, what even we
could not:

they saw us
and spared us.

On Oblivion

If, when she was sixteen, she'd hacked off her ass-length, dust-colored hair like she threatened, her friends would've clapped their hands over their mouths and giggled. The boys would've shaken their heads and called her Butch or Prairie Cactus—but she wouldn't have cared. No, she'd have started wearing her father's red-checked jacket, smoking Camels, laughing with her eyes—she'd have broken hearts.

If she'd stayed in school like she promised, she'd have been eligible for the amateur rodeo circuit that summer, barrel racing, and she'd have won at Brockton and called you. And even though you never cared for rodeos, you'd have driven hours through the dark just to sit with her on the banks of the Missouri and drink Mountain Dew until four in the morning, and maybe she'd have lain her head against your shoulder as the sun struck a new fire in the sky.

But if she'd stayed for love, you must admit, it probably wouldn't have been with you. No, he'd have been dark-eyed but taller, say six-foot-two, his blonde hair always on his ears. For the most part, he'd have said very little but surprised her now and then with things like, *This dust ain't so bad, The jackpines bend like grass in the wind, Here, let me help you with your blouse.* But too: he'd be hard to get along with Tuesdays, home from hours in the sun—always the cracked skin of his hands, always that burn of wind around his eyes.

If she'd never left Montana, her horses would still graze across the river. You'd walk to the bridge in the mornings, like you did this morning, but they'd be there, snorting, crow-hopping, offering the great flowers of their noses over the fence wire. You'd cluck to them, stroke the coarse hairs of their throats, call their names—*Franklin, Loretta, Gypsy Kisses.*

And as you say, *horses, her horses,* you wish beyond all things she would've seen someone she loves die. For then she might have understood that we are owed nothing, that the world asks permission of no one, and she might never have given herself to him, that sad and terrible man with the rainy eyes. She might've settled for the quiet boy, for morning chores and afternoon cigarettes, for every once in while rolling up her jeans and wading barefoot in the cold river beneath the stars. But she didn't. She went with the sad man. Not because she loved him but because his need of her was fiercest, his need said the world might be another way, and when she tried to leave him—you see, she always left—he shot her and buried her beneath a tangle of chokecherries.

And the east wind still pours off the prairie. And even for your shelter of years and books and marriage—you bend to it. Like the dry grass, you are broken. Breathe this dust and know that a long time ago there was a sunrise and horses—and you can turn away from nothing.

Sunday

On a two-lane highway,
somewhere south of Miles City, a boy drives
a blue diesel pickup. He's sixteen and doesn't
give a shit. His friends yell,

Faster. Faster. Fuck yes,

faster. They've peeled off their shirts. From silver cans
they gulp warm beer. It's hot as hell

(it's Sunday,
fifteen years gone, but still I see them swerve and roll
over everything—
          this house, my wife
in her garden, the tall grass by the fence giving
in the breeze),

          so he drives faster. His friends climb
into the truck bed, shake and heave full cans of beer
to the highway, where they explode, and again
explode—those shook cans,
               those stupid and lovely
boys. Now they're at the S-curves above the river,
no more highway but sky

(it's Sunday—
I'm on my knees, trying to breathe this sudden
rattlesnake of wind in the trees).

Stoploss

for Jared

In an easy chair he wakes,
                    long body
bathed in blue-dark flickerings—
                              now rises,
stands naked at the window. Below him the city steams
and creaks. There are no stars. The dumb moon leers.

Without reason he remembers running breathlessly
after his older brother—
                              veering through a bright
field of weeds into the shadow
                    of an abandoned
orchard, fruit knotted and red as fists. Who knows

if they're still there? The scarred trees, the hollow-
stalked weeds,
                    and near the ditch that wash of delicate,
yellow bones? Who knows? No one knows

anything anymore.

Sunflower River Road

for Paul

This road bends around
cane swamps, raises

a thick dust to hide
the end of day. I am sorry

for my silence, ashamed
that I have words

for this road and none
for your dying. I can even

hear the green cries
of cypress trees.

Tower of Babel

In the mountains a man lives
close to his eyes. When there is sun,
he is fat & happy
and fish bones pop in the fire,
in their little blue flames of oil—
but when the sky goes
black with storm, the bright mouths
of stars snap closed, & a man must
speak with his hands.

The eye of the radio was red,
and its round mouth was talking—

about the shadow people,
                    who live among us,

who through the grassy guts
of the country are building a highway—

                                        a thing to carry
the strange and the sorry, the muscled and the unwilling,
the rabid, the lonely, the old—

                                those with rags for clothes,
those with less than rags, with cardboard, with horse hair,
hot tar, river water,

                        acres of dung, acres of dust—
God yes they are the ones who from rusted cans eat with bent spoons,
who let the sun speak to them in the lost tongue of the first lovers,
who grow wings and walk—

                        God yes they are the ones
who from our kitchens steal the toaster, the sugar drawer, the idea
of the sugar drawer, from our lungs steal song—

                            God yes they are the ones—
who with their animal eyes and teeth like sorry stars
carry faces God yes be careful
like ours—

On the Beginning of Winter in Some
Lost Industrial City of the North River Country

Coatsleeves. Weeping brick. So the sky kicks down
its cold doors. The woman next door saying
something. *Nothing, baby. Nothing,*
he says back. *I don't know one thing*

about that. The river ice, the sky ice, a boy's face
ice-wracked: red as flowers, his blood big.
His mother? Where is she? Next door:
Baby, please? You want a cigarette? Baby? Now

like wet factory smoke the dark falling. How smoke
is evidence. How nothing's
burning. So streetlight. So black hat. Your breath
riding the wind's bad back down the pocked alley,

up the gin store's grim bricks, and up, up
the cloud-laddered sky, the stone bluffs east of town—
then to break, fade like common smoke. Up there: big
houses and burr oaks in their vestal robes of snow. Down

here: ropes of icy rain. Sumac's frozen, broken fingers. Down
here: a man opening a door into some kind of life,
saying, *Baby. Baby, I think I'll step out.*
Get me some cigarettes. You want something? Baby?

Poverty

The Reverend Elijah Love walks Highway 82
hoisting his salvation signs high overhead.

Each step is a prayer for a trucker to shift gears
and meet Jesus at that new speed, a plea

that the big woman eating at Church's
Chicken will throw her head back

and cry for mercy in a wild scatter of wings
and biscuits. Yet his own son is taken

by the devil. The Reverend knows well
the smell of sulfur and sweet melon wine. It steams

from the yellow eyes of the drunks
down Church Street. It falls from the thick,

curved thighs of Angel Williams. That stink
is on his boy. Each night the boy comes

home later, his words sour with liquor,
and the Reverend Love takes his boy

and whips him for the devil that is in him
and all the quick faces slipping so cool and easy

down these wasted streets.

Radio All Night Special AM

She wakes in the night, tunes in Chicago.

There is a song by George Jones
that too soon fades to whirrups, static. *That old devil,* her father
liked to say, *must be sharpening his teeth.* The DJ says

there is a pretty pill now to buy
to make you prettier, says there is next Friday a benefit in Sioux City
for a boy who was tackled by another boy, whose back (my goodness,
they could hear it in the stands) seized

and like wet wood snapped. Says there is of course
this war, and now a girl in the war and (does this sound right?) a man
collared, naked, on his scraggy knees. The static's back.

Be good, her father'd grin,
old devil's hungry again, then over her in the night bend for a kiss.
She spins the knob. Albuquerque. Here, at least, is always

the good news: *By the blood,*
the faceless preacher breathes, *by the blood I bind you,*
that you may not ever be unbound.

Now That It Has Been Many Years,
and I Have Moved Far from Mississippi

Say when I stepped onto that dirt road,
blackbirds did not lift from the trees like flung rags.

Say there were no snapped branches of wisteria,
no white blossoms ground into the gravel.

What harm for a moment to forget
the chill breath of the river, the boot-wetting dew,
ash dancing through the day's first spangled light.

And in the one still green corner of the lot
the cat with the fly-bitten face, strangely angled neck—
I suppose it was just old,
I suppose it was just its time,

or maybe it was only some stray image,
twisted minute of a dream,

broken bit of story I've taken
for memory. I could do it,
I think. It's like religion that way.
You simply begin

to believe: I mean it's been years.
It was way out in the country,
the weeds thick and rank.
I wouldn't find anything,
even if I went back,

not that rusted gas can,
not the ditch it was tossed in,

not that pair of child-size shoes on the front steps,
no smoke rising from their tongues,
no ash in my mouth.

Theodicy Envoy

Or how my mother hitched his blue jeans up with bailing twine,
how his snap-shirts drifted then across the bone-scape of his breast,
how for days after they fed him his yellow meal of chemical he slept on
    the easy chair in the front room, his eyes turned back into his head,
    his derelict and naked legs,
how when he finally fell back into the suffering of himself I hid in the
    chicken coop, just closed my eyes and dug my fingers into
    shit-matted straw,
like how on the television today thin-hipped young men call for god and
    murder as the tear gas comes down,
what I'm talking about is how this one day of ruin un-kins itself from all
    the rest, or how all the days are kin but vicious,
what I'm talking about is these liars my eyes, these shitty wings my hands,
    this idiot and still-charging heart,
how the little girl next door—wearing this afternoon only red underpants
    because like every other afternoon who knows where her parents
    are—screams, "Neighbor! Neighbor! Watch me fly!" and leaps
    from her swing.

The Journey

For a while he watched the sausages
turning on their heated
tumblers, the sick and viscous
swirl of nacho cheese. The lot
outside shook with heat,
fat black flies spun like trapped
birds again and again against the glass.
He bought only the necessaries—
beer, cigarettes, beef jerky.
The girl behind the counter
was maybe seventeen and slender,
her dark hair damp
at her forehead. It was very hot.

Later, near the Lightning River,
the sun sliding on its highway of bright oil
down through the darkening sky,
he could not sleep
for the heat and mosquitoes
and far below the bluff he camped on
the sad and strangled
lights of the town of Chatopa.

And in his young-man's fevered
sleeplessness he wanted
more than anything to climb down
from that miserable hill like a prophet
and beseech the citizens
of Chatopa to click off their lights
and lie down in the darkness
that was everything,
to go ahead and let the earth nuzzle

and the wet grass lick, the mosquitoes kiss
and carry them off drop by drop
into the dark, for nothing
is as good as we hope and then it's gone,
and too soon.

Yet as the first stars broke
through the black, low-hanging clouds
and a second coyote answered the call
of the first, he struck
a match for his lantern, opened a map
of Kansas, and sat reckoning
the way, the weight of hours, the rivers and hills—
the road he would drive tomorrow.

Devil's Tooth

Fireweeds are something less
than weeds: pale, rigid, not quite
green. Strange how fire
takes the pith & leaves the stem. Fireweed,
that's me: ugly in the sun,
clacking in the wind, my heart gone
up in flame. See, I need
a green star to flame between the peaks.
I need a myth that tells me, Be alive.
I need to sit awhile & think,
chew this bitter weed.

Moth

All day you've been there.
The season's late, cold wind
and colder rain. This is no place

for angelic shadows, for eyes
of ash. I know you've eaten
your fill, pulled wings

from within, made love
on the very wing of air.
And now, by my doorknob

in early winter, you wait
to die. Rest here as long as you like.
When the blue door of the moon

opens, we'll both pass through.

The Memory Eater

And I will have him rise again,
            and walk the dirt path to the machine shop—
scuff of his boots on the good earth, the sun again
on his sun-dark skin. The dark of the barn
will swallow him,
            but when I too step in he will still be there. *Father,*
I will say, and this time not be that dough-faced, fumbling boy. *Father,*
I will say, and he will turn to me,
                his good face of drought
and heavy, heaving chest, his fingers the thick-knuckled forks of sage—
and for a moment on the earth we will both us be men.
                    As swallows turn
through shit-stained rafters, as the blood eye of the sun slowly closes,
I say, *Father,* and do not know what else to say.

The Other River

I hold the river in my cupped hands.
Your dark bird lands on the arm of a cottonwood.

The water has gone black around the stumps,
track of a crow in yesterday's footprint.

I hold the river in my cupped hands.

Mostly there is mud and wind.
And the iron bones of the bridge are useless.

Your dark bird lands on the arm of a cottonwood.

Dry belly of the river studded with rocks and stumps,
and that scatter of slender bones.

I hold the river in my cupped hands.

A ton of river dust rises in the wind,
but on your back, like a bird's, it weighs nothing.

Your dark bird lands on the arm of a cottonwood.
I hold the river in my cupped hands.

Bread and Butter

I sink the shovel's rusted face
in the gravel, breathe

a bellyful of dust. Dust, sunlight,
ghosts in my mouth. Here

the good sweat
on my skin feels like scraping

meat from the hide. The old
women cluck

and turn away. I give my callouses
to the birds, who tongue

their songs in this dry air. I give
both hands, these

thick shoulders some
grandfather gave

me, to that slender, sky-eyed
boy. (See: already he has to make

fists, set his skinny self against
the wind.) I work like this

alone, shit-stained boots
and a straw hat. For lunch, I eat

dust, chew ghosts. And they fill me.

Right Now

. . . in them poems for you and me.
                            —*Whitman*

Mother, right now you're bending to your turnips,
the chapped hand of the sun on your back, that stink

of dust and horseweed and the neighbor's exploded
septic tank. Mother, right now the man on the radio

is saying *Heart,* saying *Land,* saying *Salt-of-the-earth,*
saying *Rain.* But heart, salt, rain—it doesn't matter.

Mother, you're old and getting older, that trick hip
already sewing you to the earth. Mother, right now

you're living every day of forty-years of farm work,
of dry rivers and burnt wheat, of prayers and babies,

dead men and dust—always those dead men, always
that dust. And Mother, right now I'm reading

Whitman. I'm thinking of my bright classroom,
those twenty kids. Mother, you'd like them—

they're earnest, mostly happy, even kind. But still,
at just eighteen, they've already been given more

than you ever got. And today, to top it off, they get
poems. And the spade broken turnips and good dust
and weeds, that stench of sewer that comes spilling out.

Anniversary

Three trees back of the old house,
above the bend in the river.
Out our bedroom window you
can see the third, set off from the others.
Cottonwood. Bare-branched now. I can tell you
that much. But I don't know where
they came from. Why they're here, not downriver,
or up, nearer the bridge. Who's carved what
hearts and arrows. I am not wise. I like
mayonnaise and tomato sandwiches. Sometimes,
for a week I wear the same shirt. Near sunset,
I say the hills are the color of smoke
and three-dollar wine. Sweetheart,
I have been thinking about these things. Sweetheart,
it's cold out, the very air takes my breath away,
leaves a hurt in the back of my throat. It's from all
I have done wrong. I know that. Sweetheart,
the dry limbs rattle. Beneath the ice
the river still moves.

Route 7 Outside Nacogdoches, Texas

for Liz

It is the time before you,
for some reason, that I remember most—

the Angelina River shedding its skin
of light, the cypress water dark,

a lone crow the color of highway,
color of sky. I was happy.

The music was ours
and loud—steel guitar, mouth harp, tire hum.

I lit a cigarette. A possum winked
its dark lids in the twilight.

This is about desire,
the good pain inside distance. Later,

the night gone liquor black,
radio catching miles

of static, there was only
the ache of cicadas and wind

and leaves in the wind,
and I did not know I was driving

to you. I was driving.

She Devil

You hand-over-foot the scree slope up,
goat walk the insane ridge. There's a buzzard
in these rocks, or maybe it's only
altitude. Keep walking. See Heaven's Gate
far below, your brother just ahead. Remember her,
how she held you safe above
that snow-melt flood of mountain river: fatherless
sixteen, furious boy & terrified man.
Up the scree the monarchs stream
in orange suicide. Their windy bones
won't break, but hear the music of shin, wrist,
& red-black rock, remember the fierce promise
she whispered in your ear,
the one truth: keep walking.

On the Various Examples of Manhood
I Observed in My Prairie Youth

Most were drunks or church-goers,
and save Saturday nights or Sunday mornings,
you could only tell them apart
by temperament—the church men
were louder, meaner, sure they were owed
some kind of respect or deference,
especially from the knot of grubby boys
sucking down cans of Mountain Dew
and kicking dust outside town's lone saloon.

Plain and simple, I preferred
the drunks—all stumbles and smiles,
pork rinds, salty peanuts, jokes
about goats. Consider Kelly Dempsey,
the two-toothed wonder, who one day
standing next to me at the urinals
professed his undying love
for my widowed mother and then fell ass-down
onto the piss-wet floor. Or Dom Barsilucci,
known as Old Barstooly, a blood sun
always rising in his right eye. I was on my way
to the post office when he cornered me
outside the saloon. Voice dropping
to a dusty whisper, meaty hand
working the roped scar along his jaw,
he proceeded to tell me that if I ever needed
help, the kind of help I couldn't ask
a woman for—bail money, rubbers,
the name of a guy who could get guns
or blank checks—not to hesitate. Jesus,

if he didn't mean it. What is it a boy needs
to make a man? Sometimes, I'll catch myself
fooling with the broken disposal,
still trying to impress my wife, or on the way
to Des Moines I'll slow for no reason
through one no-account town or another,
where a boy—holes in his jeans,
hands in his pockets—hunches his shoulders
against some lonesome, angry weight,
and like that it is early afternoon,
the sky shot with light, and Dom's hands
are shaking. To brace himself
against himself, he leans into the saloon's bricks,
says to me, *Now, don't go thinking*
this is some kind of ticket. I'm saying
I'll help. I ain't saying I'll be happy about it.

Anniversary

A man is looking at a picture of his dead father.
He has wondered often what it is supposed to mean,
this wide-faced man with the mustache, this man
being his father. Knowing each rise and taper
of nostril and lip, the clean dark line of the eyes.
Knowing he has just done something with his hands.
But not what. Nor what he will do in the second
following this frozen one. Not knowing how his

father will explain himself. Or to whom. Outside—
winter, a slate sky, two small birds on a bare limb
of the black walnut. One with a yellow crest, wings
of calico. The other full dark, iridescent. Outside—
birds, and blown leaves, maybe rain. Inside—
a picture of a dead man in another man's hands.

Near the End of It, or Six Little Revolutions

One

Near the end of it he woke in the night on the leather sofa in the front room. There was the light of the moon, and it was hot, and the backs of his naked legs stuck to the couch. Suddenly lucid, he blinked his blue-silver eyes and said, calmly, Sweetheart. Sweetheart, I think I'm dying here.

Two

Near the end of it she finally understood the clear force and intelligence of the term "with child," for she was with this insistent stranger, this little ice-cream tyrant, as she had been no one else. She knew her husband, the lawyer, was jealous. For he dealt with split decisions and percentage of rewards and things of that nature all day. He could only watch and catalogue (but never know) their gapmouthed dreaminess, their blood mumble of love.

Three

Near the end of it he headed west on Highway 12 and jacked the truck up to a hundred. Years later he would forget nearly everything that seemed so important at the time—the sunrise of her hair, its earth and apple smell, the cruel words he said, her astonished and broken eyes—but remember with knee-buckling clarity coming over the last hill into town, when, for a moment, his old truck left the highway. And he flew.

Four

Near the end of it she often had to blink the world back into being a dozen times throughout the day. When this quit working, she began scraping whole plates of food into the trash, speeding for no good reason, swearing at her children. She broke things just to feel the give and scatter: sticks, paper cups and dishes, a glass bottle of vinegar. She felt terrible about it all. And couldn't explain herself beyond the fact that her young husband was dying.

Five

Near the end of it he opened his eyes and for a moment could not believe the awful softness of the light on her breasts as she moved above him.

Six

Near the end of it there is the hill of a fresh grave. Near the end of it there is as well that next wet-lipped, lung-hungry breath: after my father's funeral, while the adults ate potato salad and did adult things, I ran in circles on the church lawn and wrestled with all the other boys—our clip-on ties askew, our shirttails flapping in the spring breeze. When my turn came, I pinned Cash Franzel to the cold earth in seconds. He said I was lucky. I was so happy.

Manifesto

In April, I believe only in lilac, dogwood, and wisteria—such sudden-ness and color, indecency and mess, always opening and opening, and fading, and falling away.

When I walk a city street, say, Louisville, or Tacoma, and there is the stink of creosote and iron and fried fish, I believe in creosote and iron and fried fish.

That day the sky was brass and rust, that day I drove twelve hours straight and still didn't make it out of Texas, that day I finally pulled over at a roadside grocery ninety miles from nowhere, on that day I believed above all things in cold beer.

One night when I was seventeen, Melissa pulled me into the lit skirt of a streetlight as the first snow began to fall and kissed me on the mouth, and I believed in love.

Near Ash Flat, Arkansas, along the banks of the Strawberry River, our first cross country road trip and the farthest south either of us had ever been, my twenty year old brother chased fireflies for hours.

When the half-light fades from blue to further blue, and the lake goes stone dark, and I have caught nothing all day, I believe, always, in one last cast.

One night when I was nineteen, Melissa called to tell me that she wasn't sure why but anyway it was over, and I believed in love.

That cold evening in Birmingham, lost near the steel yards, radio spit-ting static, I just kept driving.

In those first days after my father died, when my mother sat moon-
faced at the kitchen table for hours, I'd wake my little brother and
slick an iron skillet with bacon grease and fry eggs.

Leaving Spokane, everything I could possibly call mine crammed into
a short-box Chevy pickup, I believed in open windows and
wind and her dark hair in the wind.

One night when I was twenty-seven, I watched a man in a bar on the
south side of Billings, Montana, dry his eyes with his shirt sleeve
and kiss the back of his own hand, and I believed in love.

And here at my desk this morning, staring out the window down the
gravel alley, I believe in sunlight and silver leaves, the carved bark of
cottonwoods, all those hearts and arrows.

Sunrise from a Bench on Esplanade

So what's at issue, it seems, is light—
the way it slips
and tangles in the magnolia leaves,
the fire of it on a blown skin
of silver foil.

Perhaps the issue is shadow—
that man with the cardboard hat, shaking
his strung charm
of beer cans.
The way heels click
across pavement.

Maybe stone—
how it gives, and gives so cleanly:
like ice now,
but when the sun goes down,
and the music gets loud,
it burns.

Maybe wind—
the dank breath of cypress
always on your tongue.

Maybe water—
the river blue inside you.

Or earth—
delicacy of rot: chicken bones
and weeds and a shack's
broken neck.

Or all things—
cold throat of this bright morning,
those three stray dogs,
skin of your wrist
on my wrist, the light
in the leaves.

Reckoning

Wind in the blue cedars, the soap smell
                                    of lupine giving way
to the bite of smoke and wet stone. Now crickets,
frogs, the first far
                call of a coyote—

Today, I have walked many slow miles
up this creek, and caught
                    not one silver trout. So

while the last light goes on spilling
over the mountains,
                                I stand in the rank weeds,
gnats slamming my ears. There's nothing
to be done for it.

                    I lean my pole against a pine,
wing my shirt over my head, pull off my boots

                                and pants.
All my dimpled skin a pink shock
in the coming dark,
                I wade out into fast water.

                                        Now, here,
on the backs of these cold ones, these brothers
of my own bones, the river stones,
I lay my whole self down:
                    let creek water stream

across my belly, my chest, my throat—
on into the cathedral of the nostrils,

for it is no matter. There is breath
enough for rock and trout, lung and water,
blue cedar, smoke, and skin—

all these and more. The world is good.

The Old Ways Fade and Do Not Come Back

The fields forget themselves. They hold no roots. They dry and crack,
   lift like a dirt veil over your jilted face.

The corrals collapse: now they are an old man's rotten mouth, a dune of
   dry weeds, a rust-bitten water trough, that lone goat chewing nails.

The sloughs shrink back from the reeds. Snail shells burst beneath your
   boots. Waterbirds wing their awkward way to a washed sky.

And that parade of heavy-bellied swindlers, those great dark clouds—
   see how they draw tight the silk strings of their purses, hoard their sil-
   ver coins of rain. So the sky widens, goes darker, darker yet, like the
   blue and unnatural mouth of some drowned girl. Hear the wind speak
   her last nonsense: *God*, it says. *Save me*, it says. *Suckhole. Sunlight. Blossom.*

Old Art Korenko unstrings his mandolin, buries his whiskey-bottle voice
   in the brittle, cancerous bones of his chest. The dancers let go one
   another and look away. The old men hump their shoulders once more.
   The young girls steal back their kisses. The pickle jar goes unfilled,
   the spittoon unemptied, the lip of the bar unpolished.

See now your grandmother's stygian eyes, your mother's interrupted face,
   and all the host of those from your long ago childhood grown old,
   grown thick and knotty as cottonwoods, slow as oaks, willow sad,
   with their skin like the ragged skin of a pine, their phloem hearts and
   bent arms, leafy tongues telling you how thirsty, how godawful thirsty
   they've been in this dry wind.

And the dead are not trees, they are just dead. And you do not belong
   here anymore than they. For the old ways have blown from your hands
   like birds (think how your hands, watching your father as a boy, hung
   useless as bright wings), and, like the dead, here you are only memory,

you are gaze and wander, and you are free. Lift it all up, say, *I am here. And I am not here. I am of you. And not of you. Sometimes I love. Sometimes I do not. Listen: I am going to tell you about it all.* Reach down then and refashion each mother-of-pearl shell, comb weeds from the fences, fill those wide-bellied jars lip full of pickled eggs, sift from the sky the good dust of the fields.

Joe Wilkins is the author of a memoir, *The Mountain and the Fathers* (Counterpoint 2012), and a previous collection of poems, *Killing the Murnion Dogs* (Black Lawrence Press 2011). His poems, essays, and stories have appeared in *The Georgia Review, The Southern Review, Harvard Review, Ecotone, The Sun, Orion,* and *Slate,* among other magazines and literary journals. Though born and raised on the high plains of eastern Montana, he now lives with his wife, son, and daughter in northern Iowa. You can find him online at http://joewilkins.org/.

Acknowledgments - *continued from copyright page*

High Desert Journal: "Bull Mountain Elemental," "The Memory Eater," "On the Various Examples of Manhood I Observed in my Prairie Youth"
Knockout: "Poverty"
Linebreak: "Missions School, 1922: What She Remembered"
Many Mountains Moving: "Hardscrabble Prairie Triptych," "Sunday"
Mid-American Review: "William T. Phillips"
Memoir (and): "Anniversary [A long time ago now...]," "On Oblivion"
New Madrid: "Anniversary [A man is looking...]," "Fist/Boy/Man/War," "Testimonial," "Prairie Heritage Museum, Culbertson, Montana"
Northwest Review: "The Sheep Shearers"
Orion: "The eye of the radio was red, and its round mouth was talking—"
Pank: "Mother and Child Diptych," "The Other River," "Theodicy [Stars like you've never seen stars...]"
Pilgrimage: "The Journey"
Pleiades: "Drought"
Poetry Northwest: "On the Beginning of Winter in Some Lost Industrial City of the North River Country"
Redactions: "Names on the Land"
Rosebud: "Weathering"
Southern Poetry Review: "Waffle House Parking Lot, Yazoo City, Mississippi"
The Southern Review: "Then I Packed You Up the Ridge Like a Brother on My Back"
Stone's Throw Magazine: "Stoploss"
Sweet: "Near the End of It, or Six Little Revolutions"
Talking River Review: "Moth," "Moving West"
Tar River Poetry: "Now That It Has Been Many Years, and I Have Moved Far From Mississippi,";"Sunflower River Road"
Terrain.org: "Fog"; "Sunrise from a Bench on Esplanade"
Willow Springs: "Theodicy Envoy"

Poems reprinted or anthologized: "Notes from the Journey Westward" in *Best New Poets 2009*; "Then I Packed You Up the Ridge Like a Brother on My Back" in *New Poets of the American West*; "Sunflower River Road" in *The Southern Poetry Anthology, Volume 2: Mississippi* and *Bigger Than They Appear: Anthology of Very Short Poems*; and "Manifesto" in the *Sun*.

Thanks to Steve Coughlin, Lucas Howell, and Robert Wrigley for their wise guidance in the crafting of many of these poems. And—again and always—thank you, Liz.

THE WHITE PINE PRESS POETRY PRIZE

Vol. 3   *A Gathering of Mother Tongues* by Jacqueline Joan Johnson.
Selected by Maurice Kenny

Vol. 2   *Bodily Course* by Deborah Gorlin. Selected by Mekeel McBride

Vol. I   *Zoo & Cathedral* by Nancy Johnson. Selected by David St. John